Angus & Kincardineshire's Lost Railways

by
Gordon Stansfield

Laurencekirk Station.

© Gordon Stansfield, 2000
First published in the United Kingdom, 2000,
by Stenlake Publishing
Telephone / Fax: 01290 551122

ISBN 1 84033 111 9

THE PUBLISHERS REGRET THAT THEY
CANNOT SUPPLY COPIES OF ANY
PICTURES FEATURED IN THIS BOOK.

Snapshots from the signalbox at Marykirk Station, 1953.

ACKNOWLEDGEMENTS

The publishers wish to thank the following for providing the pictures in this book: Hugh Brodie for pages 1, 3, 4, 6, 11, 13, 19, 21, 23, 30, 34, and 48; the Rex Conway Steam Collection for pages 22, 24, and 43; Stuart Mackenzie for page 14; W.A.C. Smith for pages 5, 7, 8, 9, 15, 16, 17, 26, 27, 31, 35, 36, 38, and 40; Neville Stead for pages 29, 32 and 42; Neville Stead/G.M. Staddon for the front cover and pages 18 and 20; Tom Valentine for the inside front cover, pages 10, 12, 25, 28, 37, 39, 41, 44, 45, 47, the inside back cover and the back cover.

INTRODUCTION

In their heyday of the early 1900s, the railways provided a network of rail services to virtually every town and small village in Angus and Kincardineshire. It all started in the 1830s when Dundee boasted one of the earliest railway systems in Scotland and the so-called 'railway mania' of Victorian times resulted in the widespread construction of lines which in many instances were financed by small local consortiums. Towns such as Inverbervie in Kincardineshire, which was reached in 1865, and Brechin in Angus (then Forfarshire), which received its first railway service in 1848, all benefited greatly.

Today, when the motor car is the prominent means of transport for most people, it is often difficult to appreciate just how important the coming of the railways was. To the ordinary working person a whole new world was opened up, allowing travel to take place cheaply and efficiently to towns and villages which before had been completely isolated. Farming was a prominent industry in the area and here again the railways opened up new markets further afield, greatly benefiting the many local farmers.

Change affected the railways quite considerably over the years. Until 1922 the main operating companies were the North British and Caledonian.

Thereafter, until nationalisation in 1948 when British Railways came into being, the London Midland and Scottish (LMS) and the London and North Eastern (LNER) were the operators. Today, Scotrail is the provider of all local services while Virgin and the Great North Eastern Railway provide longer distance services.

In the 1920s and '30s competition from motor buses resulted in a considerable loss of railway traffic. There were many reductions in services, although many lines remained open into the 1950s. The death-knell finally came in the early 1960s when all the lines were closed except for the east coast main line between Edinburgh and Aberdeen. At one time the two counties could boast as many as 120 stations, a figure which offers a stark contrast with the eleven open today – Arbroath, Balmossie, Barry Links, Broughty Ferry, Carnoustie, Dundee, Golf Street, Monifieth, Montrose, Portlethen and Stonehaven.

It is hoped that this book will rekindle memories with many people for whom the railways were once part of everyday life. Readers should note that, even though the network has more or less disappeared, the opportunity still exists to travel the way it was by taking a trip on the preserved steam railway from Brechin to Bridge of Dun.

Drumlithie Station.

Alyth Junction (Alyth South Junction) – Dundee (Ninewells Junction)

Passenger service withdrawn	10 January 1955	*Stations closed*	*Date*
Distance	16.75 miles	Rosemill Halt	Unknown
Company	Caledonian	Baldragon	10 January 1955
		Baldovan and Downfield *	10 January 1955
Stations closed	*Date*	Lochee	10 January 1955
Newtyle (Second)	10 January 1955	Lochee West **	1 January 1917
Auchterhouse	10 January 1955	Liff	10 January 1955
Dronley	10 January 1955		

Newtyle Station, 1909.

* Known as Baldovan until September 1905.

** Known as Victoria until May 1882 and Camperdown until February 1896.

On the left is a J37 0-6-0, no. 64618, with a 'Scottish Rambler' railtour at Auchterhouse, March 1964.

This line was opened by the Dundee and Newtyle Railway in December 1831 and was unusual in that it used a 4 foot 6.5 inches gauge and had several inclines. However, these were all removed by 1860 and a new station at Newtyle was opened in 1868. The line from Alyth Junction allowed for through trains running from Alyth while at Newtyle through trains from Blairgowrie joined the line on a branch from Ardler. With the closure of the branch line from Alyth Junction to Alyth in July 1951 the level of passenger use decreased. Coupled with the closure of the Alyth Junction to Dundee Line was that of the branch line from Blairgowrie to Coupar Angus. Freight services were withdrawn during the mid 1960s, the last survivor being Lochee which lasted until November 1967.

Baldovan and Downfield Station, 1909.

A former Caledonian Railway 4-4-0, no. 54500, with a special
train for railway enthusiasts at Lochee, May 1961.

The closed station of Lochee West, January 1961.

Alyth West Junction – Ardler

Passenger service withdrawn	10 January 1955
Distance	1 mile
Company	Caledonian

This line was really a spur from the Caledonian's mainline from Stanley Junction to Kinnaber Junction. The spur left the line to the west of Alyth Junction and ran to Newtyle Station, thereby allowing services to run to and from Dundee. The services using the spur generally began at Blairgowrie and as that branch closed on the same date the need for passenger services ceased. The pattern of services which were in operation for most of the line's life were about five return workings daily Monday to Saturday.

Arbroath – Elliot Junction

Passenger service withdrawn	1 February 1848
Distance	0.75 miles
Company	Dundee and Arbroath

Station closed	*Date*
Arbroath (Lady Loan)	1 February 1848

This short line was the original Arbroath terminus of the line from Dundee which was owned by the Dundee and Arbroath Railway Company. From the north the Aberdeen Railway Company brought its line into Arbroath at its own terminus. This was in the period before a joint station was built and a horse tramway service operated the short distance between the two terminals. Both terminals closed when the joint station was opened in 1848.

Arbroath (St Vigean's Junction) – Guthrie (Guthrie Junction)

Passenger service withdrawn	5 December 1955	*Stations closed*	*Date*
Distance	7.75 miles	Colliston	5 December 1955
Company	Caledonian	Leysmill	5 December 1955
		Friockheim	5 December 1955

A former Caledonian Railway 0-4-4T, no. 55230, arriving at Colliston with the 1.35 p.m. service from Arbroath to Forfar on 3 December 1955, the last day of service.

Leysmill Station, 1924.

This route was part of the Arbroath and Forfar Railway Company's line from Arbroath to Forfar which opened to passengers in January 1839. It was subsequently taken over by the Aberdeen Railway Company in 1848. The original loading gauge of the line was 5 feet 6 inches but this was converted in 1846/47 to the normal gauge. Once the network developed Guthrie became a junction on the Caledonian main line from Stanley Junction to Kinnaber Junction which carried services from Perth to Aberdeen. At Friockheim there was a spur northwards which provided a link to the north section of the Caledonian line but this was used infrequently. Most services from Arbroath ran on to Forfar from Guthrie. When the line was being built the local laird at Guthrie objected to the railway going through his land at ground level. The problem was solved when the line was built raised on an embankment and crossed above a porter's lodge at the entrance to the grounds. This became known as the Guthrie Gate and resembled a castle battlement. Freight services along the line lasted until January 1965.

Arbroath – St Vigean's Junction

Passenger service withdrawn	1 February 1848
Distance	25 miles
Company	Aberdeen Railway Company

Station closed	*Date*
Arbroath (Catherine Street)	1 February 1848

This was the first section of the Arbroath and Forfar Railway Company's line from Arbroath to Guthrie and on to Forfar. The line was taken over by the Aberdeen Railway Company and when a joint station was opened in Arbroath to serve the lines of the Dundee and Arbroath Railway and the Arbroath and Forfar Railway this short section was closed.

Ballater – Aberdeen (Ferryhill Junction) *

Passenger service withdrawn	28 February 1966
Distance	42.75 miles
Company	Great North of Scotland

Stations closed	*Date*
Banchory (first)	2 December 1859

Stations closed	*Date*
Banchory (second)	1902
Banchory (third)	28 February 1966
Dee Street Halt (Banchory)	28 February 1966
Crathes Castle Halt	1 January 1863
Crathes	28 February 1966

Banchory Station.

* Stations on this line that were in Aberdeenshire were Ballater, Cambus O'May, Dinnet, Aboyne, Aboyne Curling Pond Platform, Dess, Lumphanan, Torphins, Craigmyle Siding, Glassel, Mills of Drum, Park, Drum, Culter, MIlltimber, Murtle, Bieldside, West Cults, Cults (first), Cults (second), Pitfodels Halt, Ruthrieston and Holburn Street.

Crathes Station, *c.* 1908.

Known as the Deeside Railway, the first part of this line opened between Aberdeen and Banchory in 1853. An extension to Aboyne opened in 1859 and to Ballater in 1866, with plans to extend the line further. To this end earth works were completed as far as Bridge of Gairn but the idea fell through. The Deeside was famous for its royal trains which carried the Royal Family to Ballater for their holidays at Balmoral Castle. In addition to these there were special messenger trains for urgent despatches from London. British Railways tried to cut the costs of running the line in 1958 with the introduction of a battery railcar, followed by diesel railcar services, but despite this the service was withdrawn in 1966.

Brechin: West Junction – East Junction

Passenger service withdrawn	1917
Distance	0.5 miles
Company	Caledonian

This short line was known as the Brechin Avoiding Line as it allowed trains running between Forfar and Bridge of Dun as well as those on the Edzell branch line to operate direct without the need to reverse at Brechin Station which was the terminal station for trains arriving from Edzell in the north, Forfar in the south and Bridge of Dun in the East. This short line was closed, not because of a drop in traffic, but because the track was required for the war effort during the First World War.

Brechin – Bridge of Dun (Bridge of Dun Junction)

Passenger service withdrawn	4 August 1952
Distance	4 miles
Company	Caledonian

Parallel with this closure was the service from Brechin to Forfar which when put together with the Brechin to Bridge of Dun service provided an alternative route on the Caledonian main line for the stations at Bridge of Dun and Forfar. Opened in February 1848, the Bridge of Dun to Brechin line was part of the plans for a Montrose to Dubton to Brechin railway which had been made as far back as 1819 when the famous engineer Robert Stevenson put forward the idea that such a route was suitable for rail traffic using inclined planes. Although the pattern of service which developed and lasted until closure was of about ten trains Monday to Saturday to and from Montrose, connections could be made at Brechin for trains to Forfar and also on the branch line to Edzell. At Bridge of Dun connections could be made for Perth and Aberdeen. After the withdrawal of passenger services a freight service to Brechin continued until May 1981. In 1979 the Brechin Preservation Society was formed and have reopened the four miles of track to Bridge of Dun on which they operate a steam service mainly at weekends in the summer months.

Brechin Station.

Brechin – Forfar (East Junction)

Passenger service withdrawn	4 August 1952	*Stations closed*	*Date*
Distance	15.25 miles	Brechin	4 August 1952
Company	Caledonian	Careston	4 August 1952
		Tannadice	4 August 1952
		Justinhaugh	4 August 1952

The staff of Tannadice Station, *c.* **1907.**

Opened in January 1895, this line had three intermediate stations which served small rural communities. At Brechin services were provided to Bridge of Dun and these were withdrawn on the same date. At Edzell Junction on the Brechin to Forfar line, trains headed northwards to Edzell. This service was withdrawn in April 1931, reinstated in July 1938, and withdrawn completely in September of that year. In 1922 there were five departures Monday to Saturday from Brechin to Forfar, stopping at all stations, with a journey time of about forty-five minutes. In the reverse direction there were the same number of arrivals except on Saturdays when there were six trains from Forfar. By 1949 there were three departures Monday to Saturday, two of these calling at all stations.

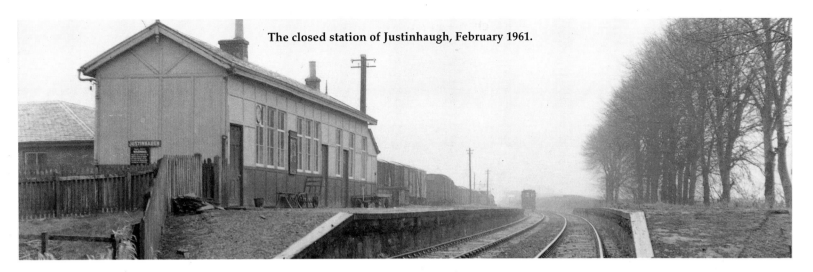

The closed station of Justinhaugh, February 1961.

Broughty Pier – Broughty Ferry

Passenger service withdrawn	1 May 1851
Distance	0.5 mile
Company	Dundee and Arbroath Joint Railway

This line was opened in May 1848. Broughty Pier was an important place at that time as the Tay Bridge had not yet been built and the pier served as a port for boats coming north from the Forth ports such as Leith. This short section of line was closed when the line was rebuilt and diverted in order to join the East Coast main line between Dundee and Aberdeen. Opened in May 1878, the Tay Bridge dramatically reduced journey times between Aberdeen and Dundee to Edinburgh (even though passengers still had to take a sea passage at North Queensferry until the Forth Bridge opened in 1890) and it also increased revenue for the North British Railway who owned it. However, events took a tragic turn on the stormy night of 28 December 1879 when the bridge collapsed, taking with it a five coach train carrying 75 passengers. The North British were partly to blame for allowing the train to cross in such bad weather and also for allowing trains to run at excessive speeds over the bridge and thereby weakening its structure. It wasn't until June 1887 that a replacement bridge was opened and until then ferries carried rail passengers between Tayport and Broughty Ferry.

Broughty Pier – Dundee (Broughty Ferry Pier Junction)

Passenger service withdrawn	19 June 1887
Distance	0.5 miles
Company	Caledonian

Station closed	*Date*
Broughty Pier	19 June 1887

Opened in May 1851, this line replaced the half mile line from Broughty Pier to Broughty Ferry and was an improvement as it allowed trains to join the east coast line between Dundee and Aberdeen in order to face the Aberdeen direction. The line was closed from 1 June 1878 until 1 February 1889 as the company did not feel that enough traffic could be generated.

Carmyllie – Elliot Juntion *

Passenger service withdrawn	2 December 1929	*Stations closed*	*Date*
Distance	5 miles	Carmyllie	2 December 1929
Company	Carmyllie Light Railway	Denhead	2 December 1929
		Cuthlie	2 December 1929
* Closed to passenger traffic from 1 January 1917 until 1 February 1919.		Arbirlot	2 December 1929

Two class 2MT 2-6-0 engines, nos. 46463 and 46464, photographed from the footplate, passing Denhead with a special train, June 1960.

This was one of the few lines jointly owned by the Caledonian and North British railway companies. Carmyllie in Angus was famous for its slate quarries and the branch line on the Dundee to Aberdeen route was built by the Earl of Dalhousie to transport slate and paving stones from the quarry. From 1865 the line was run by the Scotland and North Eastern Railway Company and subsequent changes in ownership resulted in its acquisition by the Caledonian Railway Company in 1866, followed by joint ownership with the North British Railway Company in 1880. It was not until February 1900 that the railway opened to passenger services after it was incorporated in a Light Railway Order. Freight services continued until May 1965.

The same engines as pictured on the previous page arriving at Carmyllie with a 'Scottish Rambler' railtour, April 1962. The gradients on the line were fairly steep – 1 in 36 – and to tackle them this service needed to be double headed.

Dundee East – Camperdown East Junction

Passenger service withdrawn	5 January 1959	*Station closed*	*Date*
Distance	1 mile	Dundee East	5 January 1959
Company	Caledonian		

A former North British D34 4-4-0, no. 62485, at Dundee East Station, May 1955.

The station at Dundee East was the city's terminus of the Dundee & Arbroath Joint line. It was situated at the end of a short branch from Camperdown Junction. The line handled local services from Dundee to Forfar and along the east coast route to Arbroath. Upon closure the services were re-routed to Dundee's Tay Bridge station. Freight services to the station lasted until 1967.

Dundee (Ward Street) – Fairmuir Junction

Passenger service withdrawn	8 June 1861	*Stations closed*	*Date*
Distance	1.75 miles	Ward Street	8 June 1861
Company	Dundee & Newtyle	Back of Law	July 1855

The line from Dundee Ward Street was part of a branch which ran from Dundee Harbour on the Dundee and Newtyle railway. The railway operated by the use of inclines but these were replaced by a new deviation of the route from Dundee to Newtyle. The section from Fairmuir Junction to Ward Street closed when the new deviation was provided in Dundee with new stations being opened at Liff and Victoria. The station at Ward Street was also known as Ward and West Ward. Back of Law was also known as Offset and Cross Roads.

Dundee West Station.

Dundee West – Buckingham West Junction

Passenger service withdrawn	3 May 1965	*Station closed*	*Date*
Distance	1 mile	Dundee West	3 May 1965
Company	Caledonian		

A former Caledonian Railway 4-4-0, no. 54494, leaving for Perth from Dundee West, May 1955.

Dundee West was the terminus of a variety of passenger services which arrived from the west and north west. Like Dundee East, the station was at the end of a short branch line and it was more sensible to have all services use the Tay Bridge station. This became more practical with the removal of a large number of local services. By the early 1960s, Dundee West Station only boasted about ten daily departures bound for Perth and Glasgow Buchanan Street and during quiet times the station must have seemed pretty ghostly.

Edzell – Brechin (Edzell Junction)

Passenger service withdrawn	27 September 1938	*Stations closed*	*Date*
Distance	6 miles	Edzell	27 September 1938
Company	Caledonian	Stracathro *	27 September 1938

Edzell Station.

The Edzell branch line opened in 1896 and provided a link from the small village of Edzell to Brechin where connections were available to Forfar and Bridge of Dun stations on the Caledonian main line between Perth and Laurencekirk. In the 1920s there were eight return journeys to and from Brechin, with the six and a half mile trip taking about twenty-five minutes. The whole line was closed to passengers in April 1931, but reopened in July 1938 in order to determine if there was sufficient demand for future services. Regrettably there was not and the line lost its passenger service for the second time in September 1938. After closure the line continued to handle freight including some traffic for the United States Air Force Base at Edzell and like many other branch lines in the 1960s, enthusiast specials visited the line prior to the withdrawal of freight services in September 1964.

* Known as Inchbare until 1 October 1912 and Dunlappie until November of the same year before settling as Stracathro.

Forfar (First Station) – Forfar

Passenger service withdrawn	2 August 1848	*Stations closed*	*Date*
Distance	0.5 miles	Forfar (first)	2 August 1848
Company	Aberdeen Railway Company		

Forfar's first station, operated by the Aberdeen Railway Company, was closed to passenger traffic upon the opening in the town of the Scottish and Midland Junction Railway Company's station. The Aberdeen Railway Company had leased the line from the Arbroath and Forfar Railway Company in order to reach Forfar and make a connecting junction with the Scottish Midland who had constructed their line from Perth. This route latterly became the Caledonian main line from Perth to Aberdeen which joined the present day main line from Edinburgh to Aberdeen at Kinnaber Junction.

Forfar (West Junction) – Broughty Ferry (Forfar Line Junction)

Passenger service withdrawn	10 January 1955	*Stations closed*	*Date*
Distance	17.75 miles	Gagie	10 January 1955
Company	Caledonian	Kirkbuddo	10 January 1955
		Monikie	10 January 1955
Stations closed	*Date*	Kingennie	10 January 1955
Kingsmuir	10 January 1955	Barnhill	10 January 1955

Kingennie Station, 1955.

The line from Forfar to Broughty Ferry was a direct line which linked the line from Perth to Aberdeen at the Forfar end with the line from Dundee to Aberdeen at Broughty Ferry. Opened in 1870, the line was mainly rural, although there was a certain amount of through traffic. As there were several places in Scotland called Barnhill, British Railways renamed it Barnhill (Angus) in 1952. By 1949 there were only three return workings between Forfar and Dundee with an additional one on Saturdays, and with the rapid development of bus services in the 1950s, the fortunes of this line declined. The line from Forfar to Kingsmuir lasted until 1958 while the southern section from there to Broughty Ferry remained in use until 1967.

Friockheim (Friockheim Junction) – Glasterlaw (Glasterlaw Junction)

Passenger service withdrawn	1 February 1908
Distance	0.5 mile
Company	Caledonian

This short spur was a link from the Arbroath to Forfar line which joined the Caledonian main line from Perth to Kinnaber Junction at Guthrie. The spur enabled trains to run north between the two lines, thereby allowing trains to run between Arbroath and Bridge of Dun and forming the easterly side of a triangular junction. The line was very infrequently used and latterly only had one train running over the short stretch.

Inverbervie – Montrose (Broomfield Junction)

Passenger service withdrawn	1 October 1951
Distance	13 miles
Company	North British

Stations closed	*Date*
Inverbervie *	1 October 1951
Gourdon	1 October 1951
Birnie Road	1 October 1951
Johnshaven	1 October 1951
Lauriston	1 October 1951
St Cyrus	1 October 1951
North Water Bridge	1 October 1951
Broomfield	1 February 1867

Johnshaven Station.

* Known as Bervie until July 1926.

St Cyrus Station.

Inverbervie was the most northern station on the east coast of Scotland reached by the North British Railway Company. However, the Caledonian also had running powers over the Inverbervie branch and for a few years the line saw services being operated by both companies to their own stations in Montrose. North Water Bridge was on the county boundary between Kincardine and Angus and once in the line's early days, when an obstruction was placed on the track across the bridge, the Montrose and Bervie Railway Company, owners of the line at the time, had to call in the constabularies of both counties as the exact locus of the offence was in 'limbo'. At Montrose, trains ran from Broomfield Junction to Montrose Station which is situated on the east coast main line between Dundee and Aberdeen. When the Inverbervie line closed to passengers this section remained open for a short while for trains from Dubton to Montrose which had at one time terminated at Montrose's North British station. After closure, special services visited the line, one of the last being a steam hauled excursion in 1966 organised by a local housewife. Freight services were withdrawn that year.

A J37 0-6-0, no. 64602, passing the site of North Water Bridge Halt with the daily freight train from Montrose to Inverbervie, May 1966.

Kirriemuir – Forfar (Kirriemuir Junction)

Passenger service withdrawn	4 August 1952	*Stations closed*	*Date*
Distance	6 miles	Kirriemuir	4 August 1952
Company	Caledonian		

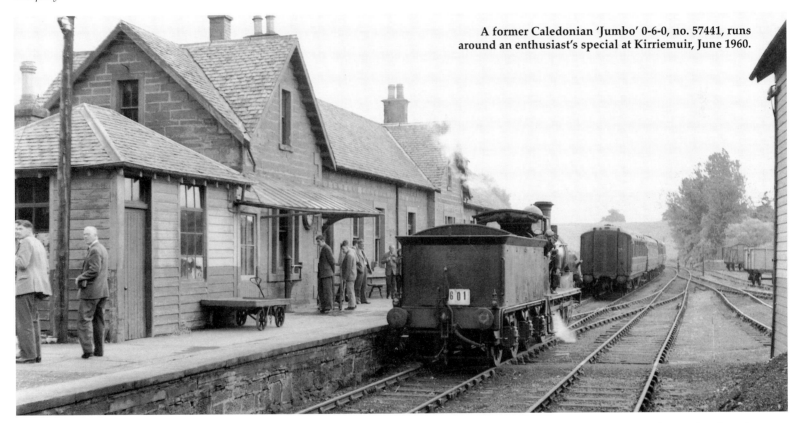

A former Caledonian 'Jumbo' 0-6-0, no. 57441, runs around an enthusiast's special at Kirriemuir, June 1960.

This was one of several branch lines which joined the Caledonian's main line between Stanley Junction outside Perth and Kinnaber Junction near Montrose. The branch was fairly easy to construct as there were no major engineering works required. It joined the main line at Kirriemuir Junction with the nearest station being Forfar. Passenger services began in August 1861 and the journey time for the six mile trip was about a quarter of an hour. Quite a number of trains on the line continued beyond Forfar to Dundee via Kingsmuir. Ten years after the line closed, the station buildings at Kirriemuir were still standing when an Easter special visited the branch. Freight services lasted until 1965 and the branch track was lifted shortly afterwards.

Montrose (Caledonian Station) – Broomfield Junction

Passenger service withdrawn	30 April 1934	*Stations closed*		*Date*
Distance	1.25 miles	Montrose (first)		17 September 1849
Company	Caledonian	Montrose (second)		30 April 1934
		Broomfield Road Junction		31 December 1878

The staff of Montrose's second station, c. 1904.

Montrose had two stations. One belonged to the Caledonian while the other was operated by the North British and was situated on the east coast main line. The Caledonian's served trains which came from Forfar and Brechin. These left the Caledonian main line between Perth and Laurencekirk at Dubton Junction, passed under the North British's east coast main line, linking with the Inverbervie to Montrose line before running into Montrose. When economies to services were being made in the 1930s it was decided to close this short branch and divert all services to the town's North British station.

Montrose's second station, long after closure.

Montrose – Dubton Junction

Passenger service withdrawn	4 August 1952
Distance	3 miles
Company	Caledonian

In the early part of 1951 passengers could board a train at Montrose's North British station and travel on Caledonian lines to Dubton and Brechin as well as to Inverbervie, but two years later both these services had disappeared from the public timetable. Opened in February 1848, these services terminated at the Caledonian station in Montrose. When their second station closed in 1934 services were diverted to the North British station on the east coast main line from Broomfield Junction which was on the Inverbervie branch. In the mid 1920s there were fourteen return journeys to Dubton with some continuing to Brechin, but three years before closure this number was down to nine. The line remained open for freight traffic until 1963.

Newtyle (Nethermill Junction) – Meigle Junction

Passenger service withdrawn	1 August 1861
Distance	1.75 miles
Company	Scottish Midland Junction

Stations closed	*Date*
Meigle Junction	1 August 1861

This link line opened in June 1838 and left the Dundee and Newtyle Railway at Nethermill Junction. However, when the line from Newtyle to Alyth Junction was opened there was no requirement for this line to carry further passenger trains.

Newtyle – Pitnappie

		Stations closed	Date
Passenger service withdrawn	31 August 1868	Newtyle (first)	31 August 1868
Distance	1.75 miles	Hatton	October 1865
Company	Caledonian		

This route formed part of the original line of the Dundee and Newtyle Railway. When a new deviation was opened in 1868 the original line, which had been opened in April 1832, was closed. Newtyle's first station was then replaced by the second.

Rosemill – Auchterhouse

		Stations closed	Date
Passenger service withdrawn	1 November 1860	Balbeuchy Foot	July 1855
Distance	3 miles	Balbeuchy Top	1 November 1860
Company	Dundee, Perth and Aberdeen Junction	Auchterhouse (first)	1 November 1860

This Tayside stretch of line was part of the route of the Dundee and Newtyle Railway which was opened in stages. This particular section opened to passengers in December 1831 and closed when a new deviation of the line opened.

Alyth Junction Station on the Stanley (Stanley Junction) – Craigo (Kinnaber Junction) line.

Stanley (Stanley Junction) – Craigo (Kinnaber Junction) *

Passenger service withdrawn	4 September 1967	*Stations closed*	*Date*
Distance	45 miles	Eassie	11 June 1956
Company	Caledonian	Leason Hill	October 1847
		Glamis	11 June 1956
Stations closed	*Date*	Kirriemuir Junction	June 1864
Ballathie	July 1868	Forfar	4 September 1967
Cargill	11 June 1956	Clocksbriggs ***	5 December 1955
Burrelton	11 June 1956	Auldbar Road	11 June 1956
Coupar Angus	4 September 1967	Guthrie	5 December 1955
Ardler	11 June 1956	Glasterlaw ****	2 April 1951
Washington	November 1847	Farnell Road	11 June 1956
Alyth Junction **	4 September 1967	Bridge of Dun	4 September 1967
Kirkinch	October 1847	Dubton	4 August 1952

A former Caledonian Railway 'Jumbo' 0-6-0, no. 57441, at the former station of Kirriemuir Junction, returning from Kirriemuir to Forfar with an enthusiasts' special, June 1960. The main line to Aberdeen is on the left.

* Stations on this line that were in Perthshire were Ballathie, Cargill, Burrelton and Coupar Angus.

** Known as Meigle until November 1876.

*** Closed from January 1917 until June 1919.

**** Closed from December 1857 until April 1881.

This line was the Caledonian main line which allowed the company to run through trains from Glasgow to Aberdeen and even further south for trains coming from Carlisle and beyond. Opened in 1848, the line began at Stanley Junction north of Perth. This was where the Highland line to Inverness began and is still in use today. The line ran through the area called Strathmore and was fed by numerous lines coming in from the north and south, most of which closed throughout the 1950s. By the early 1960s, the line was host to some of British Railways' most powerful locomotives and as there were only intermediate stations left at Coupar Angus, Alyth Junction, Forfar and Bridge of Dun, it was possible for the Glasgow to Aberdeen expresses to attain some very high speeds. When the line closed these services were diverted from Perth to Dundee and onwards up the east coast line to Aberdeen.

Clocksbriggs Station.

A former Caledonian Railway 0-4-4T, no. 55230, at Guthrie with the 2.57 p.m. from Forfar to Arbroath, December 1955.

An A2 Pacific, no. 60527 'Sun Chariot', restarts from Bridge of Dun with the 1.30 p.m. from Aberdeen to Glasgow Buchanan Street, September 1963.

Dubton Station near the village of Hillside was the junction for Montrose on the Caledonian main line.

Closed passenger stations on lines still open to passenger services

Line/Service	Edinburgh – Aberdeen *	Station	Date of closure
		Buddon ***	By 1957
Station	Date of closure	Panmure Siding	By October 1934
Esplanade **	2 October 1939	Carnoustie (first)	1900
Dundee Trades Lane	14 December 1857	Easthaven ****	4 September 1967
Craigie	3 June 1839	Elliot Junction **	4 September 1967
Roodyards	2 April 1840	Letham Grange	22 September 1930
Stannergate	1 May 1916	Cauldcots	22 September 1930
West Ferry **	4 September 1967	Inverkeilor	22 September 1930

A B1 4-6-0, no. 61245, climbs past the Esplanade Station in Dundee with the 1.00 p.m. service from Tay Bridge Station to Tayport, November 1957.

* The closed station on this line that was in Midlothian was Turnhouse; in Fife the closed stations were Donibristle Halt, Sinclairtown, Dysart, Thornton Junction, Falkland Road, Kingskettle, Dairsie and St Fort; and in Aberdeenshire there was Ferryhill.

** Closed from 1 January 1917 to 1 February 1919
*** Also known as Barry Review Platform, Barry Links and Buddon Siding.
**** Known as East Haven until 1910.

Line/Service	**Edinburgh – Aberdeen (continued)**	Station	Date of closure
		Drumlithie	11 June 1956
Station	Date of closure	Carmont **	11 June 1956
Lunan Bay	22 September 1930	Muchalls	4 December 1950
Hillside *	February 1927	Newtonhill	11 June 1956
Craigo	11 June 1956	Portlethen ***	11 June 1956
Marykirk	11 June 1956	Cove Bay ****	11 June 1956
Laurencekirk	4 September 1967	Limpet Mill	1 April 1850
Fordoun	11 June 1956		

West Ferry Station.

* Known as Hill Side until 1910.
** Known as New Mill Offset until October 1866, New Mill Siding until
December 1891 and Newmill until October 1912.

*** Reopened 17 May 1985.
**** Known as Cove until 1 October 1912.

A Standard 2-6-4T, no. 80124, arriving at Easthaven with the 6.15 p.m. local train from Arbroath to Dundee, June 1958.

On 28 December, 1906, there was a major accident near Elliot Junction when, in blizzard conditions, a stationary passenger train was hit by another engine running at thirty miles an hour tender first (i.e. backwards). Three coaches of the passenger train (pictured) were demolished and 21 passengers and the fireman of the moving engine were killed. Initially, blame for the accident was put solely on the driver of the moving engine due to the reckless speed at which his train running and because he had earlier accepted 'something to keep out the cold'. He was sentenced to five months for manslaughter but this punishment was later remitted when an inquiry decided that other factors may equally have been to blame such as possible signal failure and the poor organisation of the line and the services running on it that day.

Elliot Junction Station, August 1956.

Lunan Bay Station.

Hillside Station, *c.* **1904. A wayside station on the North British main line, on the climb from Montrose to Kinnaber Junction, which succumbed to bus competition in 1927.**

Craigo Station – according to the message on this postcard, Etta Donald and Jack Baton are on the bridge.

At Marykirk Station, 1953.

Fordoun Station, *c.* 1909.

Newtonhill Railway Station with Ocean Place behind.